SPAIN

Heather and John Leigh

Illustrated by Joseph McEwan

Designed by Graham Round
Edited by Jane Chisholm

Part 1. Guide to Spain

The name Usborne and the device ⊕ are Trade Marks of Usborne Publishing Ltd.

First published in 1980 by Usborne Publishing Ltd, 20 Garrick Street, London WC2E 9BJ, England.

Printed in Belgium by Henri Proost, Turnhout.

How to use this part of the Book

This is a picture guide filled with useful and interesting information about Spain. Take it on holiday with you, and find out about exciting things to see and do, or read it at home to find out what it is like in Spain.

The book explains some of the new and unusual things you will see. It describes what to eat and where to go, and suggests some fun things to do, such as visiting a film set where Westerns are made, watching fiestas, or playing chess with giant pieces. It makes visits to castles and churches fun by giving you things to look out for. You can find out all about shops and money, and it tells you about Spanish beaches too.

There are lots of interesting things to spot, which will make your travelling fun. When you see something, put a tick in the square next to the picture. The words in heavy type, like **this**, tell you what to tick for.

The map on page 5 shows many of the places mentioned in the book. Spanish names have been used for places and people, except where the English names are very well-known.

Some places may be closed during the winter or on certain days of the week. It is a good idea to check opening times with a local tourist office. Look for a sign saying *Oficina de Turismo,* or *Delegación Provincial de Turismo.*

Before your trip it is helpful to collect as much information as you can about the area you are going to visit. On page 61 there is a list of useful addresses and books to read. Don't forget your camera, and a notebook for recording interesting things you see.

You could make a collection of things to remind you of your holiday by saving postcards, bus and entrance tickets, menus, sweet wrappers, small coins and anything else you can find.

Facts about Spain

The official name for Spain is El Estado Español. It covers an area of 504,963km. This includes mainland Spain, the Balearic Islands, the Canary Islands, the cities of Melilla and Ceuta on the coast of North Africa, and some small islands off the coast of Morocco.

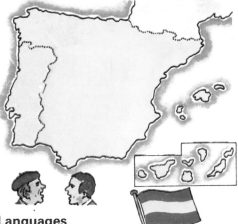

History

In the Middle Ages Spain was made up of separate kingdoms, some of which were ruled by the Moors, invaders from North Africa. In 1460 the two strongest kingdoms were united when King Fernando of Aragón married Queen Isabel of Castilla. In 1492 they recaptured southern Spain from the Moors and so united most of Spain.

The king

The head of state is King Juan Carlos de Bourbon. His heir is his eldest son, Felipe.

Languages

The official language is Castillian Spanish, which comes from a mixture of Latin and Arabic. In Cataluña many people speak the Catalán language. The Basque language is spoken in the Basque regions of the Pyrenees, and Gallego in parts of Galicia.

The flag

The red strips are said to represent the blood shed in the country's wars. The yellow represents the gold from South and Central America which made Spain rich.

The government

The government is headed by a prime minister and a council of ministers. The Spanish parliament, the Cortes, has 554 members, and is elected for four years. Spain is divided into 14 main regions, consisting of 50 provinces, each with an assembly and governor.

Main products

Spain's main crops are olives, grapes, oranges, lemons, onions, tomatoes, wheat, barley and sugar beet. Sherry and wine are major exports. Tourism is one of the most important industries.

Facts and figures

Population: 37,000,000
Six largest cities: Madrid, Barcelona, Valencia, Sevilla, Zaragoza, Bilbao
Highest mountain: Teide, Tenerife, 3,718m
Longest river: Ebro, 910km
Official religion: Roman Catholic

These islands are off
the coast of Morocco,
over 1000 km from
Spain.

CANARY ISLANDS

Public holidays

1 January: New Year's Day
6 January: Day of the Three Kings
19 March: St Joseph's Day
Maundy Thursday
Good Friday
1 May: Worker's Day
25 May: Corpus Christi

24 June: The King's Saint's Day
25 July: St James' Day
15 August: Assumption Day
12 October: Spanish Day
1 November: All Saints' Day
8 December: Conception Day
25 December: Christmas Day

Shopping, Eating and Money

When you go abroad it is fun to explore the shops to see the different kinds of things they sell. Here are some of the most useful places to shop in Spain. You can find out about smaller shops on page 8.

Some towns in Spain have large supermarkets called **Hipers** or **Supermercados**. These often have stalls outside selling hot food, such as paella.

In the centre of most towns there is a **market** where you can buy all kinds of things, including fresh fruit and fish.

El Corte Inglés, Galerías Preciados and **Simago** are department stores which have branches in many towns.

Money

Spanish money is the peseta. Five pesetas are sometimes referred to as one "duro". You can find out how many pesetas there are to the pound or dollar at any bank.

On the **1,000 peseta** note is a picture of José Echegaray, a Spanish scientist, dramatist and politician.

The **500 peseta** note shows Jacinto Verdaguer, a 19th century Catalán poet.

Eating

Cafés are open from early in the morning until very late at night. You can buy snacks and sometimes proper meals. In the evenings, people often entertain their friends in cafés, rather than at home.

Bars (also called *Tascas* and *Tabernas*) serve drinks and snacks called *tapas.* These could include olives and mushrooms or small pieces of seafood.

Look out for restaurants called **Hosterías** or **Fondas**. These serve special regional dishes and sometimes have waitresses in traditional costume.

The **100 peseta** note shows the Spanish composer Manuel de Falla.

Here are the Spanish coins. On the back they have the king's head. Older coins have the head of General Franco who ruled Spain from 1939 to 1975.

5 pesetas

25 pesetas

½ peseta

1 peseta

50 pesetas

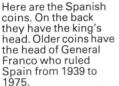

The Shops

Pastelería. You can buy cakes, pastries, and sweets here. It sometimes sells wines and spirits too.

Librería. This is a bookshop, not a library.

Churrería. A café where you can have coffee and fritters called *churros*. People sometimes come here for a late breakfast.

Farmacia. The chemist's shop. This is where you buy medicines. Look for the red cross outside.

Carnicería. Butcher's shop. The meat is usually displayed on a glass-fronted refridgerated counter because of the hot weather.

Estanco, Tobacconist's. You can buy stamps here too. Look for the red and yellow sign.

Frutería. Fruit shop. You will often see the fruit piled outside the shop.

You can often see **balloon sellers** in the street and in parks.

Tienda de Comestibles. A grocer's shop which sells fresh or tinned food, and household goods.

Droguería. You can buy perfumes and toiletries here, but not medicines.

Ferretería. The ironmonger's. You can buy pots and pans and other hardware.

Pescadería. The fishmonger's. You can see the fish displayed on mounds of ice to keep it cool.

Panadería. This sells fresh bread. You can often smell the bread being baked.

Agencia de Viajes. You can buy railway, boat or airline tickets, and book coach tours here.

Tocinería. A special pork butcher's, selling pork, ham, sausages, and cooked meats. You can see the different meats hanging from the ceiling.

Oficina de Turismo. Tourist information office. It will give you maps and details of hotels and places to visit.

Correos. Post office. You can have letters sent to you at the *Lista de Correos* in the town where you are staying.

This kiosk sells **newspapers**, **magazines** and **postcards**.

9

Food

Spanish food varies a lot from region to region. It is a mixture of Arabic as well as European styles of cooking. Here are some of the most well-known dishes to look out for.

Gazpacho is a cold soup from Andalucía. You sprinkle pieces of tomato, pepper, cucumber and fried bread into it.

Empanada is from Galicia. It is a pie filled with any kind of meat or fish as well as onions and peppers.

Paella, a speciality of Valencia, is named after the shallow metal pan it is cooked in. It is yellow saffron rice with pork, chicken, fish and shellfish.

Cocido is from Castilla, but you can find it in other parts of Spain too. It is a stew made with different kinds of meat, sausage, chick peas and vegetables.

Fabada is a thick bean soup made with pork, ham and spiced sausage. It comes from the Asturian mountains.

The **tortilla**, a potato omelette, is eaten all over Spain. Sometimes it has onions, and other ingredients too.

Trout stuffed with slices of smoked ham (*jamón serrano*) is a traditional recipe from Navarra.

Riñones al Jeréz are kidneys cooked with sherry. This dish is from Andalucía.

Calamares en su tinta is squid cooked in its own ink. You can find this in all the coastal regions.

Pollo a la Chilindrón is from Aragón It is chicken lightly fried with peppers, tomatoes and olives.

Seafood

Mussel **Crab** **Scallop**

Prawn **Lobster**

Squid **Crayfish**

Seafood is very popular in Spain. There is a good delivery service so that you can often get fresh fish inland too. See how many of these you can spot in restaurants and fishmongers.

Zarzuela de Mariscos is a spicy shellfish stew from Cataluña and Galicia.

Ingredients and flavourings

Olive oil is used a lot in Spanish cooking. Olives are one of Spain's main crops and grow mostly in the south.

In the north you may see **men travelling from door to door, selling garlic and dried peppers**. These are also common ingredients.

Breakfast

Here is a typical **Spanish breakfast**. It consists of *churros* (fritters), *buñuelos* (sugary buns), toast, butter and jam.

Puddings

Two popular puddings are **flan**, which is similar to cream caramel, and **brazo de gitano**, or gypsy's arm, a kind of Swiss roll with rum-flavoured filling.

Sweets and cakes

Spanish sweets and cakes are very sweet, especially in the south, where there was more Arab influence.

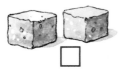

Membrillo is a jelly made from a fruit called a quince.

Yemas are egg yolk sweets traditionally made by the nuns of San Leandro, Andalucía.

Marzipan animals are often sold at Christmas, Easter and other festivals.

Drinks

Spain is famous for its **sherry** – a wine strengthened with brandy. It is named after the English pronunciation of Jerez de la Frontera, where it is made. Other countries make sherry too, but real sherry comes from the area around Jerez. There are two main types: Fino (pale and dry) and Oloroso (dark and sweet).

Spain produces many different types of wine. One of the best and most expensive is from the **Rioja** region.

Spanish children often drink **Blanco y Negro** – black coffee with a spoonful of vanilla ice cream.

Sangría is a popular refreshing drink, made from red wine, brandy, fruit, sugar, soda water and ice.

A **porrón** is a special container for drinking wine. Pour the wine into your mouth from about half a metre, trying not to spill it.

Cremat is a strong Catalán drink, made from rum, gin, coffee, sugar and lemon. It is set alight as it is served.

Horchata is a sweet milky drink, made from crushed almonds. It comes from the south-east of Spain.

Newspapers, Magazines and Crafts

Here are some different magazines and newspapers to look out for when you are in Spain.

Vanguardia, Arriba and **El País** are the main national daily papers. In Cataluña, look out for **Avui** and **Punt Diari**, which are written in the Catalán language.

There are several weekly news magazines, such as **Semana, Destino, Actualidad** and **Gaceta Ilustrada**. **Pulgarcito** and **T.B.O.** are children's comics.

Crafts

There are a number of traditional crafts still carried out in Spain. Here are some that you can buy.

Most regions have their own style of pottery. This is from Valencia.

Lace and embroidery

Hand-made Spanish **guitars**.

Basket and wickerwork

Jewellery. This is a traditional design from Toledo.

Leather goods are cheaper in Spain than in many places.

Roads and Transport

Motorways in Spain are called *Autopistas* and are marked as "A" roads on the map. Main roads, or *Carreteras Nacionales,* are marked with a red "N" on the map. *Carreteras Radiales* are special roads linking Madrid with main cities or frontiers.

Autopistas de peaje are motorways where you have to pay a toll. They were built privately and the toll helps pay for the building and maintenance. You pay the money at kiosks like this built across the motorway.

The motorways have **special service areas**. This board shows that you can buy food, drink and petrol.

There is only one brand of petrol in Spain – **CAMPSA**. It comes in three grades: normal, super and extra.

On some parts of the motorway there are **rest areas**, with trees, tables and benches and pieces of sculpture.

Signs

Warning signs are painted on triangles with red edges. This one – beware of falling rocks – is common in the Pyrenees.

All vehicles used for commercial purposes, such as taxis, display an **SP plate**. It stands for *servicio público.*

Lorries, caravans and trailers have special **numbers on the back** which show the maximum permitted speed.

Madrid and Barcelona both have an underground system called the **Metro**. Look out for this sign.

What the signs mean

CUIDADO/PRECAUTION   Caution
DESPACIO   Slow
DESVÍO   Diversion
PASO PROHIBIDO   No thoroughfare
CURVA PELIGROSA   Dangerous bend
DIRECCIÓN ÚNICA   One way street
PELIGRO   Danger
ESTACIONAMIENTO PROHIBIDO   No parking
LLEVAR LA DERECHA   Drive on the right
LLEVAR LA IZQUIERDA   Drive on the left
ESTACIONAMIENTO
DE AUTOMÓVILES   Car park

Vehicles to spot

SEAT 133. Popular two-door car. Made in Spain under licence from the Italian company FIAT.

Taxi. It has a coloured stripe down the side, and a light on the roof to show that it is for hire.

Ambulance. Usually privately run converted Citroën estate cars. Equipped for most emergencies.

Fire engine. There are several different models in use, but they are all red with blue flashing lights.

Water tanker. In some areas pure drinking water is not available. Spring water is delivered in tankers.

Butane gas delivery truck. Many families use butane gas for cooking. It comes in orange cylinders.

Trains

Spanish railways, the RENFE, operate many different kinds of trains. *Omnibuses and ferrobuses* are slow local trains. The TER, the TAF and the *Talgo* are fast trains for which you pay special supplements. On some days, *Días Azules,* you can get reductions for children. Ask at the local station.

Look out for the **Talgo**, a type of very fast diesel train built in 1950. It has reclining seats and air-conditioning. The trains are silver and have special names, such as the "Virgen de Lourdes".

Buses

Spanish **buses** are single-decked. You give the driver your fare as you enter, and leave by a door in the middle. There are few seats so most people stand.

Planes

Iberia is Spain's national airline. The planes are painted with the national colours and are all named – DC10s are called after Spanish painters.

In the Countryside

Here are some things to spot as you travel through the countryside. Some things will vary according to what part of Spain you are in. The crops that are grown depend on the climate and soil. Try to recognize the most common local crop.

In the south you will see a lot of **olive plantations** Olives grow well in areas with little rainfall.

There are **vineyards** in many parts of Spain. In September you can see the grapes being harvested.

Look out for bright yellow fields full of **sunflowers** They are grown to make oil.

In many places you can see people **threshing corn** in the traditional way. The farmer rides on a sledge pulled by horses which are treading on the corn to separate the grains.

Rice is grown near Valencia. The fields are irrigated by canals. Canal gates are opened and closed to control the amount of water going to each field.

It is quite common to see huge **advertisement hoardings** in the middle of fields. This bull is advertising a make of brandy and sherry.

Fruit

Fig

Orange

Date

Almond

Water melon

Pomegranate

Prickly pear

There are many different types of fruit grown in Spain. Here are some of the most common ones you will see.

16

Things to spot

Look out for different kinds of **windmills,** such as the ones from La Mancha (left) or the one from Cadíz (right). Some have been mechanized and are still in use.

A noria is a well with a wheel which has small buckets attached to it. A donkey is tied to the wheel. As it walks round, water is drawn up in the buckets.

In central Spain, you sometimes see **storks** nesting in the chimney pots.

In the corn-growing areas of the north, you can see **hórreos**, which are used for storing grain. They are built of stone or wicker, and stand on columns topped with flat stones, to prevent rats climbing in.

Look out for **rows of poplars** along modern or deserted roads. They were originally planted by the Romans.

You can find **religious shrines** in remote places, such as on mountain paths.

In Galicia, **granite crosses** are a common sight. Some have Christ carved on them.

Sometimes you will see **donkeys laden with special panniers** for carrying things.

Sometimes you can see **women carrying things on their heads,** such as milk churns or heavy baskets.

Heavy loads of hay or vegetables are often carried on a **cart drawn by a pair of yoked oxen**.

17

Beaches

This map shows you the different Spanish coasts, and tells you what their names mean.

Costa Verde
green coast

Costa Brava
rugged coast

Costa Dorada
golden coast

Costa de Azahar
orange blossom coast

Costa Blanca
white coast

Costa de la Luz
coast of light

Costa del Sol
coast of the sun

Canary Islands

These islands are off the coast of Morocco, over 1000 km from Spain.

Where to eat

Most beaches have a **merendero** – a stall selling drinks and ice creams.

You can often find small open-air restaurants called **chiringuitos**.

Things for hire

Many beaches have **sunshades** for hire.

Sometimes there are **beach chairs** too.

Changing tents are especially common on the north coast.

What to do

Along the Costa Brava and Costa Dorada there are tourist boats called **cruceros**. They cruise along the coasts or travel from one resort to another.

Some of these boats have **glass bottoms**. You can travel over the reefs to see the colourful fish and plant life.

You can go for **camel rides** in the Canary Islands. Some beaches have black sand. This is caused by volcanic eruptions.

On most beaches you can hire a two-seater paddleboat called a **pedalo**. This costs about 100 pesetas an hour.

You can often hire small **sailing dinghies** for about 300 pesetas an hour.

Snorkelling equipment is quite cheap to buy. Even in shallow water you may see unusual fish, plants and coral.

Windsurfing is a popular new sport, but it is not suitable for young children.

Things to spot

You often see **coconut sellers** on Spanish beaches

On the north west coast you may see **hórreos**, which are used for storing grain.

These unusual looking boats are for **catching mussels**. They have wires dipping into the sea which mussels cling to.

Houses

Traditional styles of Spanish houses vary from region to region, according to the different climate and the building materials that are available. Here are some of the main types. See how many you can spot.

In the pine-growing regions of central Spain, houses are often made from a mixture of **wood and plaster**, though the ground floor is stone. These houses are from Ciudad Real in La Mancha.

Around Valencia you can see houses called **barracas**, with steep thatched roofs. The walls are made from strips of poplar bark mixed with clay and straw.

In the south there are **flat-roofed, white-washed houses,** similar to ones in North Africa. They are made of stone as there are very few trees.

Farmhouses

Cortijos are Andalusian farmsteads. The farmer and his workforce live in a group of houses built round a central courtyard. Many of the farms are for breeding horses or bulls.

In the Basque regions, look out for **caseríos**. They are made from wood and stone and have wide sloping slate roofs with overhanging eaves. There is often a south-facing balcony. Farm animals sleep on the ground floor.

Masías are Catalán country houses with two or three storeys. The top floor is used for storing grain.

Town houses

In La Coruña on the north coast you can see **houses with balconies enclosed with glass**. This helps keep out the wind and rain. Pedestrians keep dry by walking along the arcades beneath the houses.

In the towns in the north many people live in flats in **tall narrow houses with large balconies.**

The towns in the south are sometimes called the "white towns" because the houses are whitewashed. They have thick walls and small windows to keep them cool. As there is little rain, the roofs are flat or gently sloping.

Unusual houses

In some places in the south, such as Almanzora or Guadix, there are gypsies living in **cave houses**. Notice the chimney pots and television aerials sticking out of the ground.

At Cuenca in central Spain there are some interesting **hanging houses** which are balanced on the side of a cliff. They are about 600 years old.

House Details

Most Spanish houses do not have front or back gardens. In the afternoons and evenings you often see **people sitting on chairs in the street**.

The southern houses have a **patio** in the centre, with palms or potted plants. In Córdoba there is an annual competition to choose the best one.

Houses in the south often have **pots of flowers hanging on the outside walls**. This is the Street of the Flowers in Córdoba.

Look out for decorated tiles, or **azulejos**, on the walls. Many houses have tiles on the floors too.

In northern Spain look out for **shields and coats of arms** above doorways.

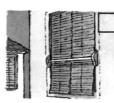

Most houses have shutters. This type is rolled up at the top of the window.

Sometimes you see **red peppers hanging from rooftops or doorways** to dry.

Ironwork

Spain is famous for its designs in wrought iron. Look out for interesting **decorated balconies**.

There is usually a **decorated iron gate** leading into the patio.

Iron bars against the windows, called **rejas**, let air in and protect the house from intruders.

Towns and Villages

There are a lot of old towns and villages in Spain. In the Middle Ages, villages were often built so that they could be easily defended. Here are some examples of different types of towns and villages you might see.

In Castilla you can often see **villages built round castles on hilltops**. The castle is probably in ruins now, but it once provided work for the villagers.

In the south there are **villages built on steep cliffsides**. This made them difficult to attack. Sometimes the rock forms the outside walls of the houses.

Some towns, such as Toledo, are **built on the bend of a river.** The river provided water and a good defence against enemies.

Walled towns, such as Avila, were built in the Middle Ages. The Avila walls are still complete. They have 88 towers and nine gateways.

Some towns have one or two old **gateways** still standing. This used to be the only way in and out of the town.

Old towns on the coast are usually **ports or fishing towns**. Cádiz was founded in 1100 by Phoenician traders from North Africa.

Sometimes you see old **villages built round a church**. Religion played a central part in people's lives and the church was often the most important building.

23

Visiting Towns and Villages

There may be a **statue** of a king or important local person. This is the explorer Pizarro, who discovered Peru.

In the centre of the oldest part of a town or village you can find a main square, usually called the **Plaza Mayor**. It often has trees and seats where people meet to talk.

Look out for different kinds of **stone crosses**.

Religious shrines are sometimes built into the side of a wall. People leave flowers and lighted candles.

Some towns have **interesting street lamps** made of decorated wrought iron.

Some houses do not have running water. So people do their washing in a special **communal washing area**.

There are often **taps or wells** in the main square. See how many different types you can spot.

Look out, too, for interesting **fountains**. Some have **carved animals' heads** with water coming out of their mouths.

As it is very hot in the south, the streets are often narrow to help keep out the sun. Sometimes a **canopy** is hung between the houses to make extra shade.

In many parts of Spain the pavement is in an **arcade** beneath the first floor of the buildings. This is a protection against hot as well as damp weather.

Look out for **paintings** and **graffiti** on the walls. This one is advertising the Spanish Communist party.

Some cafés have a **grapevine shading the tables**. It is supported by a canopy made of netting.

The local **cemetery** is usually just outside the village and surrounded by high walls.

Street sellers

In Spain a lot of things are sold in the street, partly because of the warm climate. Here are some examples.

Lottery tickets – often sold by the blind or disabled.

. **Turrón** – a kind of nougat.

A stall selling **fresh orange juice**.

Policemen's uniforms

These are the **Policía Armada**, who carry guns and guard official buildings.

The **Guardias Civiles** patrol in cars or on motorbikes, or work as customs officers.

The **Urbanos** are traffic police. Their uniforms are blue in winter and white in summer.

Prehistoric Spain

There were people living in caves and rock shelters in Spain over 30,000 years ago. Spain has lots of painted caves – mostly in the Cantabrian Mountains in the north and along the Mediterranean coast. Find out at your local tourist office which caves you can visit. There are a number of other prehistoric remains to see too.

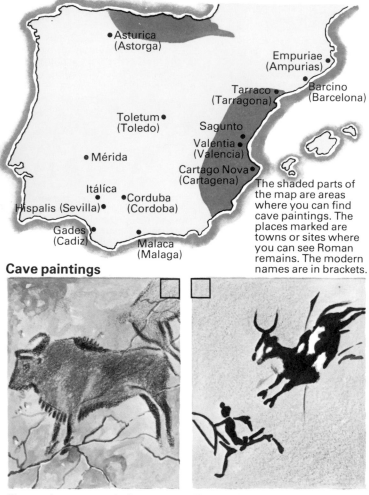

Asturica (Astorga)

Empuriae (Ampurias)

Tarraco (Tarragona)

Barcino (Barcelona)

Toletum (Toledo)

Sagunto

Valentia (Valencia)

Mérida

Cartago Nova (Cartagena)

Itálica

Corduba (Cordoba)

Hispalis (Sevilla)

Gades (Cadiz)

Malaca (Malaga)

The shaded parts of the map are areas where you can find cave paintings. The places marked are towns or sites where you can see Roman remains. The modern names are in brackets.

Cave paintings

The **northern cave paintings** are the oldest. Some are 30,000 years old. They show the animals people used to hunt – deer, boar and bison. The most famous caves, at Altamira*, are closed.

The **cave paintings on the east coast** are about 12,000 to 15,000 years old. These show human figures and scenes, such as hunting. This is known as the "Second Hunter" style.

*You can see reproductions of these paintings, see page 40

Cave signs and symbols

Here are some of the signs and symbols found drawn in the caves.

The **Indalo**. This symbolized a legendary giant from the region of Almería.

The **Tectiform**. This may have been a symbol for a building or animal trap.

Outlines of human hands. These were found in some caves.

Dolmens are tombs made from large stone slabs. There are several of these in the region of Antequera. This is the Cueva de Menga, near Antequera.

Prehistoric **weapons and tools** were made from hard stone called flint. **Jewellery** was made from shells and teeth with holes bored in them.

Iberian Spain

The period of about the last 1,000 years BC is known as the Iberian period. Archeologists have discovered sculptures, painted pottery and elaborate gold and metalwork. The Iberians traded with the Phoenicians from North Africa, who brought Greek, Egyptian and Syrian goods with them. The Celts came to Spain in about 700BC and the Greeks in about 500BC, so archeological finds show many different styles.

The **Dama de Elche** is one of the most famous pieces of Iberian sculpture. You can see it in the Prado Museum in Madrid.

The Iberians also made carvings of animals. These are the **Bulls of Guisando**, at El Tiemblo, near Avila.

A lot of **gold jewellery** has been discovered in the south of Spain. It is thought to have come from the legendary city of Tartessos.

Roman Spain

The Romans invaded Spain in 218BC. They built roads all over the country and many modern roads follow the same routes. They set up irrigation systems and worked mines. There are a number of Roman remains to see. On page 26 there is a map showing where the best sites are.

At Itálica near Sevilla, are the remains of a large **Roman town**. It was the birthplace of the Emperor Hadrian. You can see where the streets and houses used to be. There are some mosaics and the fourth largest amphitheatre in the world.

Roman theatres were semicircular. The best-preserved theatre is at Mérida, where plays are still performed. The stage consists of a set of marble columns with statues between them.

Amphitheatres were round arenas surrounded by seats. Here the Romans used to hold chariot races and gladiator fights.

The Romans invented the arch, which meant they could build stronger, higher bridges. There are several **Roman bridges** in Spain. This one is at Alcántara.

Aqueducts were used to carry water from one place to another. The Segovia aqueduct, built in the 1st century AD, is 300 metres long and brought water from the Sierra Fonfría, 14 kilometres away.

Roman temples were elaborately carved. This one at Mérida was dedicated to Mars, the god of War.

Roman arches in Spain were usually built in memory of an important person. This one is at Medinaceli.

Mausoleums were burial places for rich people. This one at Fabara was dedicated to the spirits of the ancestors.

Cemeteries were always built outside towns. The Tower of Scipios, near Tarragona, is the tomb of a noblewoman.

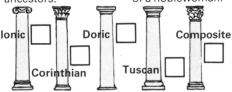

Ionic   Doric   Composite
Corinthian   Tuscan

In some towns you can see the remains of **Roman walls**, though often they have been added to at later periods.

These are the five different types of **columns** used in Roman architecture. See how many you can spot. The Ionic and Corinthian were originally Greek, and the Doric was adapted from the Greek version.

Mosaics are pictures or patterns made from small coloured stones. They were used to decorate floors. Some are scenes from everyday life, others show legends.

Look out for Roman remains in local museums. They may have **coins, pottery, statues or ornaments** that have been dug up in the area.

29

Moorish Spain

The Moors were Muslims from North Africa, who came to Spain in 711AD and ruled parts of the country until 1492. They brought science and maths skills and introduced paper and also the numbers we use today. They also planted orange and lemon trees. You can still see Moorish style architecture, especially in the south.

The **Alhambra** is a Moorish city built on a hill in Granada. It includes two luxurious palaces, which were begun in the 12th century. Between 1236 and 1492 the Alhambra was the capital of Muslim Spain. You can visit it on any day of the week.

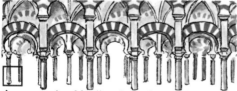

A **mosque** is a Muslim place of worship. This one at Córdoba was the most important in Spain. It is now a cathedral. Notice the horseshoe arches and stripes of red brick and white stone. These are typical Moorish features.

The Moors built beautiful **gardens** with pools and fountains. These are the gardens of the Partal in the Alhambra.

Look out for **minarets** – towers for calling people to prayer – which were built next to mosques. This one is the Giralda in Sevilla.

Spotting Moorish styles

Moorish ideas had an influence on building styles in Spain. Churches built by refugees from Muslim Spain are called "Mozarabic". Buildings constructed by Muslim craftsmen after the Christians reconquered Spain are known as "Mudejar".

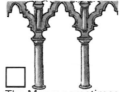

The Moors sometimes used overlapping **multifoil arches**. These are made up of lots of little arches.

Some churches copied **Moorish ceilings with parallel ribs**. Sometimes the ribs overlapped to form a star shape.

The Moors often built in **brick**. Look out for brick churches and other buildings, especially in Castilla and Aragón.

Mudejar craftsmen built **belfries** that looked like minarets. Some are decorated with patterns in brick and coloured tiles.

Decoration

The Moors carved intricate designs in the plaster on walls. The Koran, the Muslim holy book, forbade the representation of people or animals. Patterns were based on **geometric shapes** (left), **plants** (centre) or **Arabic writing** (right).

Carved wooden ceilings are called **artesonados**. You can see this elaborate "honeycomb" ceiling in the Alhambra.

Moorish walls and floors were sometimes decorated with **mosaics** made from pieces of coloured pottery, or **tiles**. Many modern houses have similar tiles.

Some Moorish words are still used in Spain. Look out for **words beginning with "A" or "Al"**, such as alcázar, meaning castle. These often have Moorish origins.

Churches

Here are some of the different styles of churches you will see in Spain, and some clues to finding out how old they are. They are often a mixture of styles as they have been added to at different periods. Old Spanish churches are often well preserved because of the mild climate.

Asturian (700s–800s) Narrow with round arches. Found in the province of Asturias.

Mozarabic (800s–900s) Built by refugees from the Muslim parts of Spain. Look out for the horseshoe arches.

Romanesque (1000s–1100s) Thick stone walls with towers. Round arches on doors, windows and vaults.

Route of the pilgrims

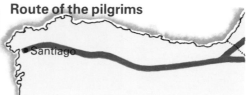

Santiago

You can see a lot of Romanesque churches along this road. It was the **route of the pilgrims**, who came from France to visit the tomb of Santiago (St James). This pilgrimage was one of the most important in the Middle Ages.

Gothic (1100s–1500s) A lot of cathedrals, such as Burgos (above), were built at this time. Tall, with a lot of windows and spires. Pointed arches.

Baroque (1590s and 1600s) Very elaborate style. Many older churches, such as the cathedral at Santiago de Compostela (above), were rebuilt with Baroque fronts.

Parts of a church

Mozarabic horseshoe arch

Romanesque round arch

Gothic pointed arch

Many Spanish churches have **richly carved doorways**. This is the Portico de Gloria at the cathedral of Santiago de Compostela.

In the 1500s walls were often decorated with delicate carvings. This style is called **Plateresque**, as it looked like the work of a *platero*, or silversmith.

Romanesque barrel vault. Rounded with a series of arches.

Gothic rib vault. Tall arches meeting at a point.

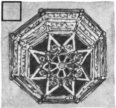

Stellar vaulting. 1500s dome with star shape made from thin strips of stone.

In some Romanesque churches you can still see **frescoes**, pictures painted straight onto the wet plaster of walls. These are from San Isidoro, León.

Stained glass windows

Stained glass windows, often showing scenes from the Bible, were introduced in the Gothic period. See how many different shaped windows you can spot.

Things to spot in Churches

In the 16th century Spain was very wealthy because of the gold and other treasures brought back from South America. A lot of this wealth was spent on churches, which are often highly decorated inside and have elaborately carved objects, such as statues. Here are some things you could look out for when you visit a Spanish church.

The **coro**, or choir, is where the priests pray. Notice the carved wooden seats, called choir stalls.

The entrance to the *coro* often has an iron grill, or **reja**. Some are painted with gold leaf and have intricate designs.

A **reredos** or a **retablo** is a painted or carved screen at the back of the altar. Many of these are enormous.

Some churches have a collection of treasures, such as **jewelled crosses**, or cups called **chalices**.

Rich or famous people often have **carved tombs**. Look out for unusual poses. This knight is reading a book.

Decorated chests are usually used for storing valuable things, or vestments – the clothes that priests wear in church.

Sometimes you can visit the **crypt**, an underground room beneath cathedrals and large churches.

Cloisters are covered arcades round a courtyard. You can find them in churches that were once attached to monasteries. Spanish cloisters are often decorated with carvings of saints or scenes from the bible.

Castles 1

Spain has about 1,500 medieval castles. There are a lot in the region of Castilla, which was named after the word *Castillo,* meaning castle. Here are a few of the castles you can visit. They are usually open every day from 9 a.m. to 1 p.m. and from 3 p.m. to 7 p.m.

Segovia Castle looks like a fairy-tale castle. It dates back to the 12th century, but was mostly rebuilt in the 19th century. You can visit the throne room, the royal bedrooms and an armoury, where you can see old canons, lances and crossbows.

The **Alcázar at Almería** is an Arab fortress, begun in the 8th century. It once housed 20,000 men. You can see a ruined palace, gardens, baths and dungeons.

The **Castle of Loarre** in Huesca dates back to the 11th century. It was the home of an order of fighting monks and the nobles who they fought for.

Belmonte Castle is a 15th century castle built by the Marquess of Villena. It is six-sided with lots of circular towers. Inside there are elaborate ceilings.

Coca Castle is a very ornate 15th century Moorish Style castle, made of pink brick. It was built as a home for the archbishop of Sevilla.

Castles 2

Most Spanish castles were built between the 8th century, when the Moors invaded, and the 15th century, when Spain became united under King Fernando and Queen Isabel. The style of a castle varies according to when it was built, though they were often added to at different periods. Here are some examples of different types of castles and some features to look out for.

Moorish castles date from the 8th century. Many have square towers and sharply pointed battlements. This one is at Almodóvar del Rio.

Early castles in the south (800s–1100s) usually have an inner and an outer wall, with square or many-sided towers. They are made of stone, brick or cement mixed with pebbles.

Early Christian castles in the north copied the ones in the south. They are made of rubble, which was the only material available, and the towers are round or semicircular.

Most **14th and 15th century castles** were built by nobles who wanted to protect their land from the king. You can usually find them in strong positions on hilltops. They fit the landscape and so are irregular in shape.

Fortified palaces, such as Manzanares el Real, date from the middle of the 15th century. These were built as homes rather than places to be defended, and are often highly decorated, outside as well as inside.

Things to spot in castles

Bartizan turret. Small round room sticking out from top of wall or tower. Used for watching for enemies.

Machicolations. Holes beneath the battlements through which things could be dropped on enemies.

Loop-holes. Narrow slits in walls through which arrows could be shot while the archers remained safe.

  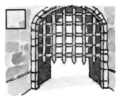

Wall-walks are walk-ways behind the battlements, which connect the towers.

Drawbridge. A bridge across a moat which could be raised from inside as enemies approached

Portcullis. Strong iron gate which slides up and down. Used for blocking the entrance to a castle.

Wedge-shaped towers. These were introduced by the Moors and can be found in south and central Spain.

Look out for **noble coats of arms** carved on the walls.

The insides of castles were often decorated by Mudejar craftsmen. Some have **elaborately carved ceilings**.

Castles you can stay in

Keep a look out for **armour and weapons** on display.

Some castles have been converted into **Paradors** – hotels run by the government. You can find out about these at your local tourist office.

Madrid

Madrid became the capital of Spain in 1561. It is built on a plateau 654m above sea level in the centre of the country. The summers are very hot and the winters very cold. A small river, the Manzanares runs through the city. Madrid has over three million inhabitants.

The **Arco de Cuchilleros** is one of the entrances to the square. Here is the sign of the restaurant "Cuevas de Luis Candelas", named after a famous highwayman.

In the 16th and 17th centuries, heretics were burnt in the **Plaza Mayor** by the Spanish Inquisition. It was also used for plays and pageants. People used to watch the events in the square from their balconies.

The Puerta del Sol is the centre of the old city. There is a **statue of a bear and tree**. They are the symbols of Madrid.

Outside the police headquarters in the square is the **Kilómetro Cero**, the point from which all distances in Spain are measured.

In the **Plaza de España** is a monument to the popular Spanish writer Cervantes, and his two best-known characters, Don Quijote and Sancho Panza.

The **Puerta de Alcalá** was built in 1778 in honour of Charles III. A tax on wine was raised to help pay for it.

The Spanish parliament, **the Cortes**, was built in 1850. The bronze lions were made from the metal of enemy cannons.

The **Cibeles Fountain** in the Calle Alcalá shows Cibeles, the Greek goddess of fertility, riding a chariot drawn by lions. It was built in the 18th century.

The **Calle Alcalá** and the **Avenida de San José**, or **Gran Vía**, are the two major shopping streets. Look out for Grassy's jewellery store which has a clock museum.

The **Rastro** is a busy open-air market, selling antiques, junk, toys and old clothes. You can find it on Ribera de Curtidores Street.

On Sunday mornings there is a **stamp collectors market** in the Plaza Mayor.

The **Church of San Jerónimo** built in the 16th century, is where many royal marriages have taken place.

The Post Office, or **Palacio de Communicaciones**, is a huge building, a bit like a cathedral. People often meet here.

The **university** is built in enormous grounds just outside Madrid. It was modelled on an American campus.

Places to visit near Madrid

The **Escorial** is a very large palace and monastery 49km from Madrid. It was built by Philip II after his victory at the battle of St Quentin in 1557.

Franco is buried at the **Valle de los Caídos**, a memorial to the Spanish Civil War. There is a church carved inside the hill.

What to see and do in Madrid

The Royal Palace

The **Royal Palace** was built for Charles III on the site of a castle which was burnt in 1734. On a few days it is closed and used for state ceremonies.

There are luxurious rooms to visit, such as the **throne room**. You can also see a museum of old carriages, an armoury, the crown jewels, and an old pharmacy.

Interesting museums

The **Prado*** is one of the world's greatest art museums. It has a lot of famous paintings by Spanish artists, such as the one on the right.

This is the **Maids of Honour** by Velázquez.

The **Museo de América*** has a collection of toys, dolls, masks and other things that the Spaniards brought back when they invaded South and Central America.

The **Archeological Museum*** has reproductions of the cave paintings at Altamira, which are 30,000 years old.

The **Colon Wax Museum*** has figures of famous people and scenes from fantasy and horror stories. Some of them have special sound and light effects.

You can visit the **Royal Tapestry Factory*** and watch tapestries being made. It was started in 1721 and Goya created many of the original designs.

You can see old coins and banknotes at the **Money Museum***, which is above the mint where money is actually made.

The **Museo del Pueblo Español*** has costumes and old household objects from different regions of Spain.

You can visit the 4th century BC **Debod Temple***. It was rescued from Egypt to stop it being flooded when the Aswan Dam was built.

At the **Railway Museum*** you can see interesting models of old trains.

You can see a collection of old weapons and armour at the **Army Museum***.

The **Naval Museum*** has model ships, old maps and instruments used on board ship.

Parks

The **Retiro Park** was built by Philip II. It has fountains, rose gardens and a huge lake for boating.

Casa de Campo is the biggest park in Madrid. It has a zoo, a huge wood, a lake, and a funfair.

You can travel to the funfair by **cable car** from Paseo del Pintor Rosales street.

The **Botanical Gardens** has 30,000 species of plants and trees from all over the world.

Barcelona

Barcelona is the capital of Cataluña and the second most important city in Spain. It is the largest port and a centre of banking, publishing and industry. The city was founded by the Carthaginians from North Africa about 1,700 years ago. The oldest part is nearest the sea and is known as the "Gothic quarter". The "Ensanche", or modern city, was designed in the last century by Cerda, an engineer, who also designed part of Stockholm in Sweden. Here are some suggestions of things to see and do in Barcelona.

The **cathedral**, which lies in the centre of the Gothic quarter, dates back to the 13th century. At midday on Sundays, local people gather outside to dance the Sardana, a traditional Catalán dance.

The **Sagrada Familia** church, designed by the Barcelona architect Gaudí, was begun in 1884 and is still unfinished. It is sometimes called the "Sandcastle Cathedral".

The **Plaza de Cataluña** is the centre of Barcelona. It has fountains, statues and a flower clock.

The 19th century **Gran Teatro del Liceo** is the second largest theatre in the world, after La Scala in Milan.

This is the **Palacio de la Diputación**, which was the old parliament when Cataluña was a separate kingdom.

In the **Plaza Nueva** you can see Roman pillars and a building with designs by the Spanish artist Picasso on it.

The **Ramblas** is a wide tree-lined avenue that runs from the waterfront to the city centre. It has open-air stalls which sell flowers, books, newspapers and caged birds.

In the **Plaza Real** there are some unusual street lamps designed by Gaudí. Stamp collectors meet here on Sunday mornings.

The **Plaza del Rey** is a historic square where it is said that King Fernando and Queen Isabel received Christopher Columbus on his return from America.

The waterfront

You can go by lift to the top of the **Columbus memorial** for a good view of the harbour.

Between 9 a.m. and sunset you can go on board a replica of the **Santa María** – the boat in which Columbus sailed to America.

In the port area, the **Barceloneta**, you can see lots of different boats, and people mending fishing nets.

You can go for **trips round the harbour** in special sightseeing boats.

What to see and do in Barcelona

There are two mountains in Barcelona – Montjuich and Tibidabo. You can travel to the top of them by **funicular railway**.

They both have **funfairs** which are open all the year round.

On Montjuich you can explore the **Pueblo Español** – an artificial village which has styles of architecture from all the regions of Spain. It was built for a world exhibition held in Barcelona in 1929.

Inside the village there are lots of small craft shops where you can watch **potters and glass-blowers** at work.

For a good view of the old part of Barcelona you can travel by **cable car** from Montjuich to the port.

Montjuich park has lots of unusual fountains. This illuminated one is lit up on Sundays and public holidays.

Some travel agencies in Barcelona organize **donkey rides** (*burro safaris*) and trips into the country on horse and cart (*tartana*).

Güell park is a fairy-tale park designed by Gaudí. It is full of strange-shaped buildings, pillars and mosaics.

Ciudadela Park has lots of different kinds of sculpture, such as the lady and the umbrella fountain and a stone mammoth.

Inside the park you can find **Barcelona Zoo,** which has a good collection of unusual animals, such as the white gorilla "Snowflake"

Interesting museums

The **Picasso Museum*** has the world's largest collection of pictures by the Spanish artist Picasso.

The remains of ancient Roman Barcelona are on show in the basement of the **Museo de Historia de la Ciudad***

At the **Museo de Indumentaria*** you can see all kinds of costumes from the 16th century to the present.

The **Museo de Cera*** has wax models of famous people from history and fiction. This is General Franco.

You can see guns, toy soldiers and uniforms at the **Museo Militar*** in the old fort on Montjuich mountain.

The **Maritime Museum*** is inside a shipyard which was built in 1378 and is the oldest in Europe.

*You can find out the addresses on page 61.   **45**

Sports and Bullfighting

Football

Real Madrid have won the European Cup six times. The **players** usually wear all white.

Football is the most popular spectator sport in Spain. Matches are held on Sunday eveings between October and May. This is **Santiago Bernabeu**, the home stadium of Real Madrid, Spain's most famous team.

This is the **club emblem.** *Real* means Royal. King Alfonso XIII gave them this title in 1920.

Long distance cycling races go on for days and attract large audiences. One of the most famous is the Vuelta a Cataluña, which starts in Barcelona.

Pelota is a fast moving Basque game, played in a court called a frontón. There are four players. Each has a curved basket, or *cesta,* to throw and catch the ball. Spectators bet on the winners during the match.

Rowing regattas are held on the north coast. The boats are stronger and more difficult to steer than the ones used for river racing.

Sports you can do

Skiing is very popular. The main areas are the Pyrenees, the Guadarrama mountains, the Sierra Nevada mountains, and Manzaneda in Galicia.

In most tourist areas you can hire **tennis** courts for about 200 pesetas an hour. In other parts of Spain you may need to join a private club.

You will need a licence if you want to go **fishing**. To apply for one, ask at the tourist office, or at the local branch of ICONA, a conservation organization.

Spain has many good quality **golf** courses. Some are used for international tournaments, such as the Canada Cup, and the Eisenhower Trophy.

Bullfighting

The bullfight or **Corrida** takes place on Sunday evenings. The origins of bullfighting go back to legends of the Persian god, Mithras, who killed bulls.

It is performed in several stages. There are six bulls and three main bullfighters, or matadors, who wear brightly coloured, embroidered costumes.

Festivals 1

There are lots of festivals, or fiestas, in Spain. Even the smallest villages have one. Most of them celebrate religious feast days. People sometimes wear traditional costumes, and there are fireworks, processions, bullfights and dancing in the streets.

Easter

Holy Week, the week before Easter, is celebrated all over Spain. On **Good Friday**, statues of saints or scenes from the crucifixion are carried through the streets on floats, or *pasos*, lit by candles. The processions in Sevilla (above) are especially famous.

These men are called **Penitents**. They belong to "brotherhoods", which originate from the medieval trade guilds. Each brotherhood has its own colours.

Many of the **statues** are very valuable as they are decorated with jewels. The Virgin of the Macarena (above) was carved in the 17th century.

In Alberique, you can visit the **statues in people's houses**. They are taken from the church for Holy Week. Visitors are welcome for a drink and a *buñelo* (a bun).

On **Easter Saturday** in Cataluña you may see young people in the street singing and collecting money or sweets. They often have baskets and a decorated donkey.

Other religious festivals

Corpus Christi in June is celebrated in many towns. At Sitges, people make patterns in the streets with flowers. Prizes are given for the best designs.

On Assumption Day (15 August) a religious play, **the Misteri**, is performed at Elche. Singers and musicians strapped to a cable are lowered from the church dome.

Assumption Day is celebrated in other towns too. The fiesta at La Alberca lasts about four days, with dancing and a street play.

Verbenas take place the night before a religious feast. There are fireworks and buildings are strung with ribbons and flags.

Romerías are picnic outings to a saint's shrine. They are held in country districts. The most famous is to El Rocío at Whitsun. People arrive on horseback or in white covered wagons decorated with flowers. They sing and play the guitar and castanets.

Festivals 2

The **Fiesta of San Fermín** is held in Pamplona from 6 to 15 July. Each day there is the *Encierro*, when bulls run through the streets to the bullring. People run ahead to prove their courage. Most years somebody is injured.

There are several fiestas in which **mock battles between the Moors and the Christians** are acted out. They are mostly in southern Spain. One of the most famous is at Alcoy on 23 April.

At **Christmas** it is traditional to eat *turrón* – a kind of nougat made from honey and almonds.

On **New Year's Eve**, to bring good luck, it is the custom to eat 12 grapes as the clock strikes midnight – one for each chime.

Spanish children receive their presents on **6 January**. They leave their shoes out on the balcony the night before.

In Madrid and some other towns there is a **parade of the three kings,** who ride camels or horses through the streets.

The **Fallas of Valencia** are held from 12 to 19 March. People make huge figures or scenes from wood, rags and papier-mâché. The figures are usually of topical subjects or caricatures of local politicians or well-known people. On 19 March, the best one is chosen and the rest are burnt.

Some towns, such as Sevilla (above), have **Ferias**, which were originally horse or cattle markets. People wear traditional costumes, and there are parades of horses and carriages. Some people hire *casetas* – small enclosures – for private parties.

In September there are **fiestas of the vendimia**, or grape harvest, in grape-growing regions. These men are treading the grapes in the traditional way.

Many large towns have a **summer festival**. All kinds of events are organized, including music, sport, tree-felling competitions and gazpacho tasting.

Things to look out for at Festivals

During a fiesta, people often give each other small presents. There are **street stalls** selling toys, sweets and small gifts.

At many fiestas there are **Gigantes** (giants) or **Cabezudos** (huge papier-mâché heads). They often represent people from history. These ones are of King Fernando and Queen Isabel.

In the Basque region you may hear **Bersolaris**. These are men who shout mock rhyming abuse at each other from opposite sides of the street.

Costumes

Here are the head-dresses from some of the regional costumes. They are often worn at fiestas. See if you can spot any of them.

The traditional **mantilla** and comb from Andalucía.

Embroidered bonnet from Cáceres.

Peinata from Valencia.

Veil from Almería in southern Spain.

Hat and veil from Logroño in Castilla.

Straw bonnet from Tenerife, Canary Islands.

Music and Dancing

The **Flamenco** dance is from Andalucía and is probably of Gypsy or Arabic origin. It is usually accompanied by the guitar and castanets.

Tuna singers are students who sing and play the guitar or mandolin at fiestas, and in restaurants and hotels. They began in the 16th century and wear the costume of that time.

In Cataluña you may see **Castellers**, who perform a dance by standing on each other's shoulders to make a tower.

This is the **Aurresku**, a Basque dance. Each dancer tries to leap higher than the others.

The **tamboril**, a side drum, and the **txistu**, a kind of flute, are Basque instruments.

On 21 and 22 July at Anguiano in Logroño, you can watch people doing a **stilt dance**.

The **Jota** is a lively dance which comes from Aragón. It is rather like a jig.

The **gaita** is a small version of Scottish bagpipes, played in north-western Spain.

In Cataluña, in the summer, you can watch **Sardana** dancing competitions.

Fun Things to do 1

At **Tabernas**, near Almería, you can walk through the streets of sets used to make cowboy films. This is a very arid area with dramatic scenery. There are huge cracks in the earth and hardly any trees or plants. It is often used for Westerns and films set in the desert, such as *Lawrence of Arabia*.

Touring sherry cellars

In the region of Jerez de la Frontera, you can go on **tours of the bodegas,** or cellars, where sherry is stored. You can see the processes used for making sherry and sample some different types. To find out about tours contact the local tourist office.

In September, when they are harvested, you can see **grapes drying** in the fields on straw mats.

This is a **grape-press**. Years ago grapes were pressed by men trampling on them wearing special boots.

To sample the sherry the glasses are filled with a **venencia**, a bendy piece of bone with a silver cup.

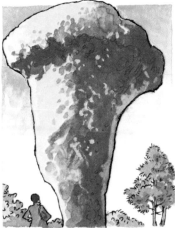

This is the **Enchanted City** near Cuenca. Weather has worn away the rocks and left strange shapes. Many of them have names, such as "the elephant" or "the man's face".

In the main square at Olot in Cataluña there is a **huge chess board** with giant pieces. The pieces are kept in a wooden box at the edge of the square and anyone can play.

You can see into the garden of **Salvador Dali's strange house** at Port Lligat, Cadaqués. There are all kinds of sculptures, including giant eggs and faces. Dali is a famous Spanish painter.

There is a very unusual tree at Icod on the island of Tenerife. It is called the **Dragon Tree** and is supposed to be 3,000 years old. There are a few other trees like it, but not as old.

Things to watch

In the evenings, in fishing towns such as Garrucha in Almería, you can watch **fish being auctioned** to the shopkeepers and the public.

At midday on Thursdays outside Valencia Cathedral, the **Water Tribunal** meet to solve disputes concerning the watering of crops. This custom is 600 years old.

Fun Things to do 2

There are several exiting **caves** to visit in Spain. The Drach (or Dragon) caves in Mallorca are among the most famous limestone caves in the world.

They are nearly three kilometres long. You enter by boat from the sea, and there are coloured lights so you can see the stalagmites and stalactites.

Fun ways to travel

You can go by **cable car** to the top of the Teide volcano in Tenerife, and see small puffs of white smoke coming from the crater.

At Benidorm and some other towns on the coast a few **steam trains** have been restored and painted, and you can go for rides along the old tracks.

At Mijas on the Costa del Sol you can hire a **donkey,** or *burro,* taxi, though it can be expensive.

In some towns, such as Sevilla, you can go for sightseeing trips in an old-fashioned **horse and carriage**.

From Pontevedra you can hire a **boat to the island of Ons.** The people there speak the Gallego language.

Watching people at work

Many factories and craft workshops will let you come and watch people at work. Sometimes you have to arrange your visit in advance, which you can do at the local tourist office. But keep a look out for small craft shops. They will usually let you in without an appointment.

In the region of La Mancha, you can often see women sitting out in the street **making lace**.

In Toledo you can visit a workshop where they make **steel goods**, such as knives or swords, decorated with gold, and black.

Potters are often happy to let you watch them at the wheel or painting designs on the pots.

At Easter time you can watch **bakers** making castles, spaceships and all kinds of shapes from chocolate.

At Manacor on the island of Mallorca you can visit a factory where they make cultured **pearls**.

In most parts of Spain you can still find workshops where there are people **weaving** on hand-operated looms.

Circuses

Look out for posters advertising travelling **circuses**. They usually perform in the local bullring which has a canopy put up over it.

Funfairs

There are mobile **funfairs** that travel round the country too. They usually come to a town when it has a fiesta.

Fun Things to do 3

Parks

In the **Botanical Gardens in Valencia** there is a play area with a roadway which has an old railway engine, a tram and other machines to play on. There is also a small zoo with monkeys.

At Elche near Alicante you can see the only **palm forest** in Europe. Look for the amazing "Imperial Palm" which has seven arms.

National parks

Parques Nacionales (national parks) are areas of beautiful countryside where animals and plants are protected. There are eight of them in Spain. This is the Aigües Tortes Park.

At the **Covadonga National Park** there is a wide variety of animals including bears, wolves, wild cats, squirrels, badgers and foxes.

At **Rioleón Safari Park***, near Vendrell, Tarragona, you can see wild animals roaming free, and performing lions and dolphins. You can go tobogganing on a special slideway too.

Interesting museums

There are lots of museums to visit in Spain. In most areas you can find an archeological museum or a museum of the history of the region or town. Here are some of the more unusual museums you could visit.

In the Romantic Museum at Sitges, there is an interesting collection of toys, called the **Lola Anglada collection**. It includes dolls from all over the world, dating back to the 17th century.

At the **Falla Museum** in Valencia, you can see the best Fallas* from each year. Fallas are papier-mâché models made every year for the feast of St Joseph.

Also in Valencia is the **National Pottery Museum** where you can see brightly coloured pottery and tiles. This is a reconstruction of an old Valencian kitchen.

The **Casa de Dulcinea**, El Toboso, Toledo is a museum about Don Quijote, who was invented by the Spanish writer Cervantes. Quijote wore armour and fought windmills because he thought they were giants.

There is a **wine museum** at Vilafranca del Penedés. It shows wine-making equipment from the time of the Ancient Egyptians. You will be given a glass of wine to try at the end.

At Vitoria is the unique **Museo de Naipes**, which is a museum of playing cards. The cards come from all over the world and some are over 500 years old.

At the **Pontevedra Museum** you can see an exhibition about hórreos. Hórreos are now used for storing grain, but some very old ones were the homes of the ancient Celts, over 2,000 years ago.

*For more about Fallas, see page 51

Car Number-Plate Game

The first letters on Spanish car number-plates tell you which province they come from. As you spot the letters, colour in the map.

A	Alicante	GE	Gerona	P	Palencia
AB	Albecete	GR	Granada	PM	Baleares
AL	Almería	GU	Guadalajara	PO	Pontevedra
AV	Ávila	H	Huelva	S	Santander
B	Barcelona	HU	Huesca	SA	Salamanca
BA	Badajoz	J	Jaén	SE	Sevilla
BI	Viscaya	L	Lérida	SG	Segovia
BU	Burgos	LE	León	SO	Soria
C	La Coruña	LO	Logroño	SS	Guipuzcoa
CA	Cádiz	LU	Lugo	T	Tarragona
CC	Caceres	M	Madrid	TE	Teruel
CE	Ceuta	MA	Málaga	TF	Tenerife
CO	Córdoba	ML	Melilla	TO	Toledo
CR	Ciudad Real	MU	Murcia	V	Valencia
CS	Castellón	NA	Navarra	VA	Valladolid
CU	Cuenca	O	Oviedo	Z	Zaragoza
GC	Las Palmas	OR	Orense	ZA	Zamora

Useful Addresses

The Spanish National Tourist Office (S.N.T.O.) will supply lists of hotels, *paradores,* campsites and details of tours. They also provide leaflets about different towns and provinces of Spain. There are also booklets telling you about winter sports, golf, fishing and other things to do on holiday in Spain.

Spanish National Tourist Office, 57 St James St, London SW1. tel: (01) 499 0901.

In U.S.A.:
589 Fifth Avenue, New York, N.Y. 10017. tel: (212) 759-3842.

In Canada;
60 Bloor Street West, Suite 201, Toronto 5, Ontario. tel: (416) 961-3131.

For general information on Spain, you can contact the **Spanish Institute,** 102 Eaton Square, London SW1. tel: (01) 235 1485.

Guide books and phrase books

The *Michelin* green guide, the *Blue* guide and *Fodor's Spain* are all good basic guides to Spain, listing interesting things to see and place to visit in the different towns and regions. Some other guide books are listed below.

You will have much more fun on holiday if you can speak some Spanish, so it is a good idea to take a phrase book too.

Letts go to Spain (Letts)
Discovering Spain (Harrap)
Costa del Sol and Andalusia (Berlitz)
Costa Dorada and Barcelona (Berlitz)
Madrid (Berlitz)
Junior Guide to Spanish (Usborne).

Museums

Colon Wax Museum, Paseo de Calvo Sotelo, 41, Madrid. tel: 419 22 82
Army Museum, Mendez Nuñez, 1, Madrid. tel: 221 67 10
Railway Museum, San Cosme y San Damián, 1, Madrid. tel: 467 34 91
Archeological Museum, Serrano 13, Madrid. tel: 226 68 32
Prado Museum, Paseo del Prado, Madrid. tel: 468 09 50
Royal Tapestry Factory, Fuenterrabia, 2, Madrid.
Naval Museum, Montalbán, 2, Madrid. tel: 221 04 19
Debod Temple, General Fanjul Gardens, Madrid.
Museo de América, Avenida de los Reyes Católicos, 6, Madrid.
Money Museum, Doctor Esquerdo, 36, Madrid.
Museo del Pueblo Español, Plaza de Marina Española, Madrid.
Museo de Cera, Rambla de Santa Mónica, 4, Barcelona. tel: 317 2649.

Picasso Museum, Calle de Montcada, 15, Barcelona.
Museum Militar, Montjuich Castle, Barcelona.
Maritime Museum, Reales Ataranzanas, Puerta de la Paz, Barcelona.
Museo de Historia de la Ciudad, Casa Clariana-Pardellás, Plaza del Rey, Barcelona.
Museo de Indumentaria, Palacio del Marqués de Llío, Calle de Montcada, Barcelona.

Zoos and Safari Parks

Zoo Municipal de Fuengirola, Camino de Santiago, Fuengirola, near Málaga.
Rioleón Safari Park, Albiñana, near Vendrell, Tarragona.
Auto Safari Andaluz, Finca La Alcaidesa, San Roque, Cádiz.
Jardín Zoologico y Botánico 'Alberto Durán', Jardínes de Tempul, Jerez de la Frontera.

Index